D.F. Gregory was born in 1968, and brought up in the historic Yorkshire village of Hatfield. He graduated from the University of Huddersfield in 1999 with a Bachelor of Arts honours degree in history before moving to London for further study and work.

He later returned to the north of England to become a family carer to a terminally ill parent with dementia. In May 2007 he became an elected town councillor, and despite suffering a physically debilitating and disabling brainstem infarction in 2015, he continued in this role later being appointed mayor twice before retiring his seat in June 2022. His literary pursuits became a relaxing pastime, assisting in his stroke rehabilitation, and later graduating into a passionate interest resulting in this publication.

To the memory of my beloved mother, Jeanette

D. F. Gregory

Collection of Poems

Austin Macauley Publishers
LONDON · CAMBRIDGE · NEW YORK · SHARJAH

Copyright © D. F. Gregory 2023

The right of D. F. Gregory to be identified as author of this work has been asserted by the author in accordance with sections 77 and 78 of the Copyright, Designs and Patents Act 1988.

All rights reserved. No part of this publication may be reproduced, stored in a retrieval system, or transmitted in any form or by any means, electronic, mechanical, photocopying, recording, or otherwise, without the prior permission of the publishers.

Any person who commits any unauthorised act in relation to this publication may be liable to criminal prosecution and civil claims for damages.

A CIP catalogue record for this title is available from the British Library.

ISBN 9781398455559 (Paperback)
ISBN 9781398455566 (Hardback)
ISBN 9781398455573 (ePub e-book)

www.austinmacauley.com

First Published 2023
Austin Macauley Publishers Ltd®
1 Canada Square
Canary Wharf
London
E14 5AA

Table of Contents

National and Patriotic 9
I Passchendaele, 1917 11
II Bannockburn, 1314 13
III Magna Britanniae 15
IV Red Dragon's Princely Roar 17
V Ode to God's Own 18
Reflective, Sentiment and Faith 20
VI Tea and Sympathy 21
VII Abide with God 22
VIII Is This Life? 24
IX As the World Walks By 25
X The Spectre of Dementia 26
XI Searching for Answers 27
XII Vivid Reflections 28
XIII The Mockingbird Sings a Sultry Tune 29
XIV As I Grow Older 30
XV Guiding Star 31
XVI Don't Quit! 32
XVII The Last Waltz 33
XVIII My Beautiful Place 34
XIX Moving On 35
XX Yearning Siren of Sin 37
XXI Two Hearts Wed 39
Environment and Humanity 40
XXII Thin Ice 41
XXIII Peace 43
General 45
XXIV A Winter Night's Tale 46
XXV The Parish Meeting 48

XXVI Morning Train	*49*
XXVII The Green Wood	*50*
XXVIII Birds at Play	*51*
XXIX Purring Puss	*52*
XXX Camelot	*53*
XXXI Merry Men of Sherwood	*55*
XXXII Exam Fever	*56*
XXXIII The Highwayman	*57*

National and Patriotic

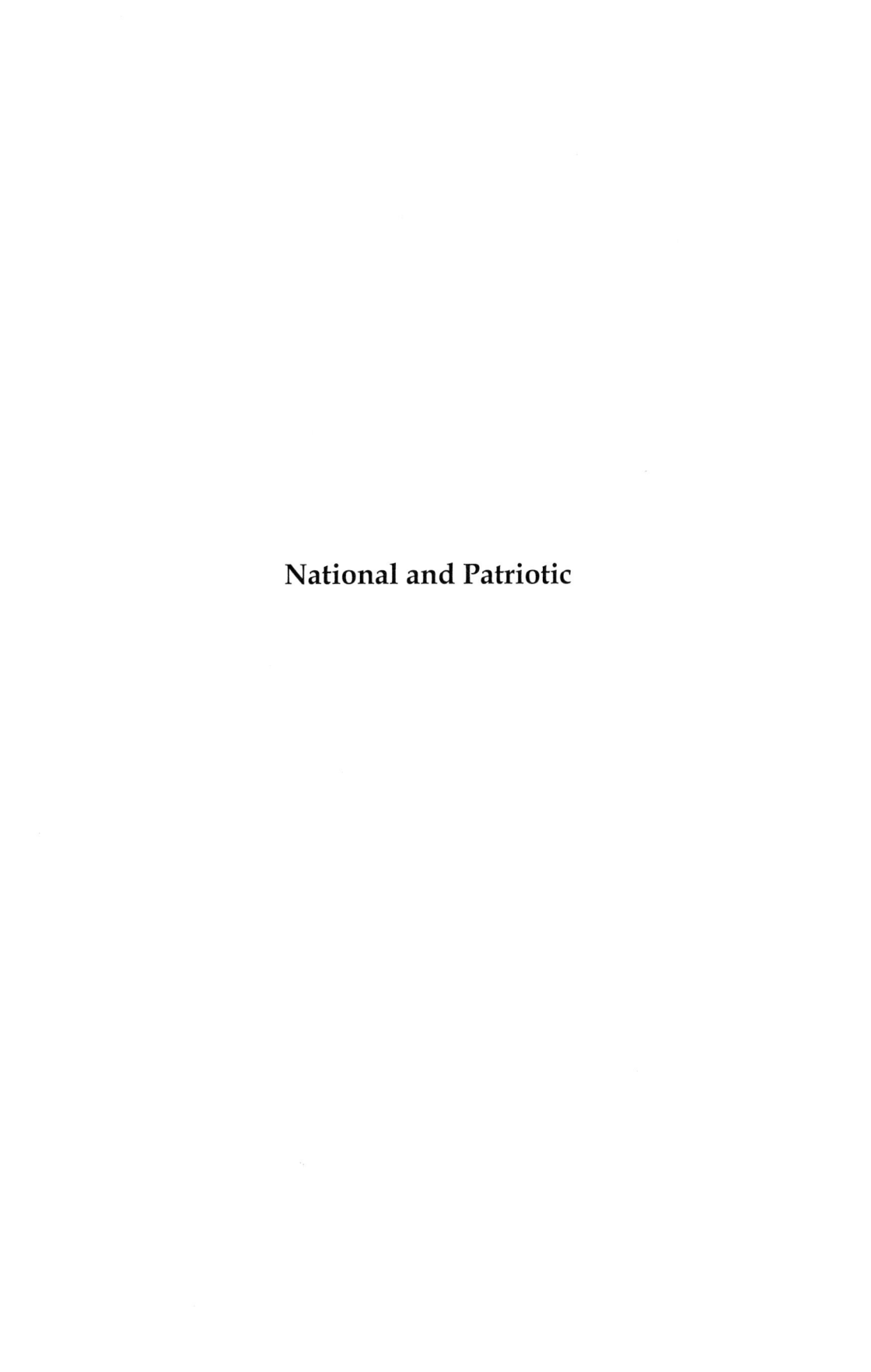

I Passchendaele, 1917
The Third Battle of Ypres

Passchendaele.
The sweat and mud, the toil and pain,
the waterlogged dig-outs and the drench-soaked trenches.
This was Passchendaele!

Sweet memories as vivid as Tommy's muddied boot print,
crust and crumble away under the sun's deadly drying ray.
Blisters on sore limbs puss and lice in follicles furrow,
fleas fester and rats scurry along the way.
Heavy hearts cling on to hope,
ghostly memories mist the air of Passchendaele.

The stale air, the cannon-smoked sky,
the smell of blood, the smell of sweat.
The stench of the Passchendaele dead,
where light foot lads were mercilessly made into men.

There be no passion on Passchendaele,
but the sweet scent of loving memories.
Homebound thoughts do linger,
misting the mind with vivid tender verse.

As the birds glide free high above,
they catch the sight of tear glazed eyes.
Nestled within their trenches they balance hope with despair,
the battled drained lads of sodden Passchendaele.

Passchendaele's churned landscape,
of combat-filled fields,
Passchendaele's terrifying machinegun and cannon shell scar,
of enduring barrage, of horrific countenance, of rot, misery and decay.

In the war that was said to end by Christmas,
Britain's fair sons' hurry, where yesterday's corpses now lay.
Flanked by their allied brothers,
shoulder to shoulder they defend the day.

This dark and dismal deluge,
this place, this bloodied place, named Passchendaele.
Passchendaele!
Where hearts fell and men were broken,
where God's serene blue skies, saw seas of blood flow.

This was Passchendaele!

II Bannockburn, 1314
Blàr Allt Nam Bànag

Outnumbered by some three to one,
Bruce's men stood firm upon Bannockburn!

Edward the Second with armies abound,
knights at ready, and archers poised proud,
stood equal in defiance awaiting the charge to war.

Armed and defiant, before an English king.
Scots stand proud with their kin,
before the Bruce, their looked-on king.

The clans' amassed, banners aloft, arms displayed!
For independence and a rightful crown,
they lay waiting their fate at Bannockburn!

Battle anew since Longshank's stand of 1298,
Falkirk's first battle for Scots independence,
now to Bannockburn's field awaits the fate!

Now the Bruce,
crowned king but eight year before,
against Edward II did stake to set the score once and for all!

Mass was said, to woo the Scottish force.
This their crusade, for independence,
make or break!

Robert and Edward looked on with defiance,
and then came the cry:
"Lay on! Lay on!"
Shouted the Scots, under English arrows on high.

The English fell that day at Bannockburn,
and fateful Edward from the shadow of Stirling to Dunbar did flee.
A Scottish dynasty was set in stone,
and a crown raised high over a Scottish throne!

> … This bonny fair land, the green of the Thistle, that is Scotland!
> … This jewel of a stone be the throne, that the Scots be proud to call Scone!

III Magna Britanniae

King John bent to the barons in 1215.
The Magna Carta was born and our laws set seed,
upon that fair field at Runnymede.
Windsor's pastures fragrant and green,
saw England's tide turn that June day in 1215!

Upon these great shores, Britannia since sits firm.
Mother of justice, equity and the free,
upon her seat her sceptre rules fair,
over sea, land, sky and law to bear!

Too plentiful to chart is old Britannia's wealth,
of histories so abundant, one can but start to tell.
Battles for crowns lay land to waste,
from Bosworth to Blackheath,
the blood flows thick and true!

In 1483 Richard the Third became king,
but by Henry VII's hand lay slain two years on,
time does pass and another era anon!

Good King Harry in 1520 lay truce,
with the French side by side, a 'cloth of gold' he produced.
Never countenanced by man before,
the opulence, the splendour, a stately accord!

By his behest a new church was founded,
and reform and emancipation was grounded.
Though divisions apparent a nation stood firm,
alone yet together she did affirm!

Queen Elizabeth's 'golden speech' of 1601 did tell,
to her Commons amassed at Whitehall she addressed.
She spoke with passion and courage,

and with a lion's heart gave it her best.
And the love for her people was manifest!

Queen Bess passed away in 1603,
laying way to a new line of Stuart's.
With change and autonomy,
James I set a seed and Charles II lost his head!

Cromwell with tyranny and tumult set his mark,
the Commonwealth laid the foundation for accountability by man.
Then after debate and battles fought,
came Charles II in '60 to public applaud!

Britannia received William and Mary — *circumitus Gloriosus!*
And then came a long eighteenth century,
of enlightenment and ingenuity.
Furnishing Britain with trade, commerce, and all.
Hail! Britannia, an empire cometh to thy shores!

Victorian industry and reform did thrust forth,
upon us a revolutionary emancipation,
of enterprise and reward.
The wheels of time turn ever more,
history reinventing at every dawn!

But Britannia remains seated firm,
grasping her olive leaf of truth and peace,
surveying her shores and skies above.
Her dominion sits firm, resolute, and in her we trust!

This Britain, this land, fulfilling from Pennine to shore.
This England, this Scotland, this Ireland and Wales,
from corner to corner be proud to applaud!

IV Red Dragon's Princely Roar
Cymru

From Conwy to Cardiff the principality stands proud.
The Welsh poppy, heather and bilberry on her pastures adorn.
But in her heights, the red dragon does roar!

The pearl-grey peaks of her mountainous fortress stand high.
Snowdon to three kingdoms, surveys the skies.
The mist upon her majestic summits, as a dragon's breath doth soar!

Slate and coal, she be industry rich,
a fair land in song, in harmonious accord.
The hills and mountains muffle the sounds of historical struggle,
serenely she stands proud!

Her history as rich as any tapestry woven,
Owain Glydŵr awaits yet to be woken.
Below and above her castles, her spirit breathes fire!

The fire in the breath of the dragon,
mighty, majestic and free.
This land of princes, known to her sons and daughters… as Cymru it be!

V Ode to God's Own

Bleak beauty!
Crisp charm!
Perilous paradise!
Wistful wonder!

The morning rays of the dawning sun
Cast a golden sheen over the heather-clad moor
The breeze whistles a faint tune
As the Peregrine is poised to pluck its unsuspecting prey

The clean crisp waters of the spring beck flow
Grazing sheep of the rolling dales
Chew the fertile green cud under the blue sky
Which like an unblemished silk sheet looks down from on high

The shepherd up at dawn
As his forefathers before
Upon this hard land countered with beauty adorned
Tends his flock with diligence dedication and thought

Glacier cut gorges
Evocative aspects
The majesty of escarpment and landscape views
This fair land that I am proud to call home

Upon this fair land
Hearts have grown dear
Upon this ancient beauty
Man has toiled and endeared

In these dales my heart grows fond
In these dales my heart grows strong
This is Yorkshire my home and God's own
For which no other I could surpass nor behold

This is where my soul belongs
From my first to my last
Where I find my peace

Reflective, Sentiment and Faith

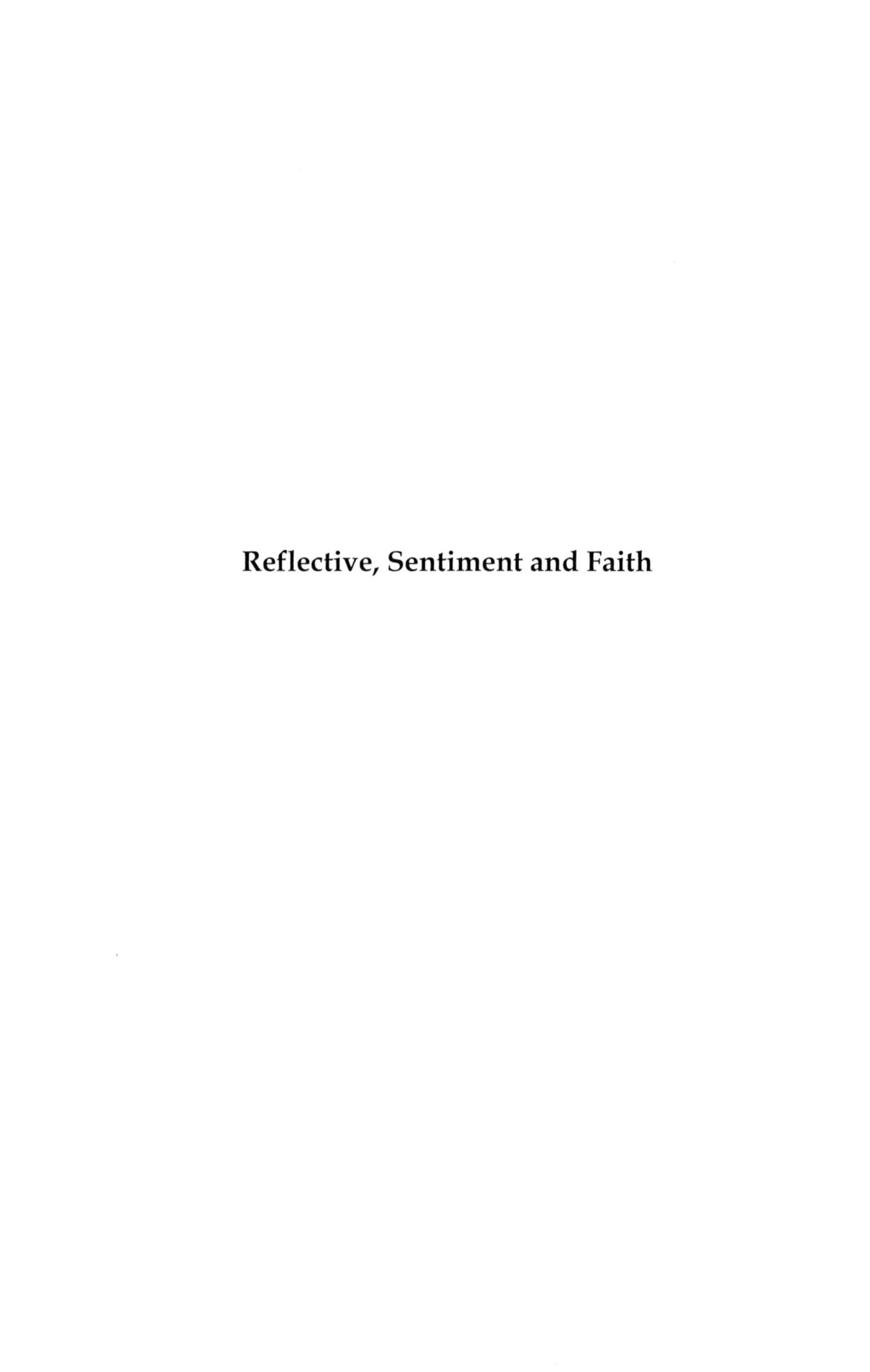

VI Tea and Sympathy

Sat in the garden under a spring blue sky,
church bells peel out a hymnal tune, the evening sun retires!

Voices in the distance over walled garden sound,
intrusively yet faintly break through my serene surround!

Birds twitter gaily and in conversation sing aloud,
motor vehicles in distant traffic groan their dulcet sounds!

Upon the table are laid tea and biscuits for a guest,
roses from the garden, it's the 23rd of April so red and white are best!

My guest arrives at six o'clock and the doorbell chimes,
the tom cats sat on the wall and the spaniel laid on the grass,
the scene is set!

I offer Chai or Darjeeling and pour the tea from the pot,
his mood surely can't be so droll as he chose the spicier Chai,
then he tells me his lot, such woe!

By the time he's finished I'm deflated and ready for something stronger than Chai,
Oh, what sorrow and tears could tell,
I Know I had a smile an hour ago!

He left much happier and with a smile,
I'm left with cold tea, a bowl of pots, and a scowl!

The cat and dog are oblivious in their little worlds,
The sun's gone down and the birds retire,
night creeps in and it's time for bed.

Sweet dreams!

VII Abide with God

I rise with the fresh morning dew,
I blossom under the sun's guiding light,
and trust in God's love all day through!

In the new day of my life,
I shall strive to be worthy,
to love, and honour and be true!

As I walk the fields, the hills and the streets,
I will walk with You,
one by one, step by step, and true!

In the noon of my life,
I shall serve Your word in all that I do.
To remain, in faith, and be true!

When I approach the evensong of my life,
I shall be unchanging.
But shall come to Your word,
follow Your command, to be just and true!

As the sun sets on my life,
I shall ask for Your blessing.
Seek Your solace,
and pray to rest with You!

In countenance of my life,
I shall look to my service.
Look into my heart,
and hope I've been true!

For You are my love,
and Your word is my rule.
The breath of life You have given,
it warms me through and through!

Now with my Saviour I lay my rest,
content with my lot that I've done my best.
Await His claim, await His judgement,
having fulfilled my calling at His behest!

At peace with Him, I surrender my soul,
not a more worthy master nor friend I could behold.
I hope I've been true and loved all my life through!

VIII Is This Life?

Is this life worth living for?
The fun, beauty, fragrance and joy!
Such a life is worth living for.

Is this life worth caring for?
The sentiment, compassion, family and friendships!
Such a life is worth caring for.

Is this life worth loving for?
The beauty, emotion, care and passion!
Such a life is worth loving for.

Is this life worth being jealous for?
The time it ferments, wastes, corrodes and destroys!
Such a life is laid to waste.

Is this life worth killing for?
The devilment, depravity, decay and destruction!
Such a life is at best put to rest.

IX As the World Walks By

In my garden chair below the ivy-covered wall,
I sit enthroned.
Sun-in-splendour, cream tea and scones,
and birds sing harmoniously in sweet tones.

Heat shimmers in the breeze like a quivering faint film
in the air,
I am content hidden there.
Butterflies pass, bees they hover,
and the squirrel jumps from a branch to go undercover.

Walkers pass by talking along the pathway,
I secretly listen at what they say.
A dog barks, the cat leaps from a wall,
But I am quite content sat with my tea and thoughts.

I sit in my garden in a chair the warm sun adorns me,
as the breeze sifts through my hair.
I sit carefree and close my eyes,
oblivious to the world passing by.

In solace I rest,
I contemplate,
I meditate,
As the world walks by!

X The Spectre of Dementia

This cruel spectre that robs the soul,
this deadly curse, this deadly demise, by dementia it's known.
Like a stormy sea battering an old wooden ship,
or the chef pulling the pork joint to shreds.
It eats its victim away, cell by cell, until the unsuspecting victim
turns to gel.

A decade I've watched the slow demise,
its torrid effects, and the pain it shares on those lookin' on.
But still I look on, and see hope through my despair,
the love, the memories, and the life we shared.

A smile beams out from within the shell still left,
a smile I knew well, with a tender caress.
A smile that will live on in my heart and soul,
never to fade, but to grow and grow old!

For love never dies nor sweet memories fade.
These are the treasures that I will take to my grave!

XI Searching for Answers

The discus moon shines a mellow light,
the blue skies darken, until night creep in.
Within the wood, a sinister place to be,
still the birds chirp, within the warm summers air,
I gather my thoughts, they comfort me.

I walk through the wood, along the pathway,
I venture bold like.
An owl dips low, spookily and silently it perches,
yet under the stars, warm air and the scents,
I gather my thoughts, they comfort me.

I feel no hast, no fear within,
as I walk through the wood guided by the moonlight glint.
I sit on the grass, under an oak tree, close my eyes and be at one and
in peace,
I gather my thoughts, they comfort me.

I countenance my achievements and regrets, what I have done and left undone.
Is there still time or have I had my day?
Does my fate behold providence my way?
I look to the stars and I gather my thoughts, they comfort me.

Not to know whether it could have been or will be,
if I had done different, or not, as the case may be.
I sigh a deep breath and my conscience lies still,
I look into my soul, will my answers fulfil?
And I gather my thoughts, they comfort me!

I open my eyes and all is still,
I feel content, renewed and fulfilled.
The silent night surrounds me and all is serene,
my thoughts they be answered?
I be calm and content, reassured and heartened… Comfort I feel!

XII Vivid Reflections

As the sun shimmers upon the water surface,
sweet little ripples dance in the breeze.
In tune my heart beats to every passing memory.
So sweet, so sweet!

My mind plays games and with my heart it wrestles,
endearing memories and melancholy tangle a web.
But deep in my heart fond thoughts reflect.
So endearing, so endearing!

The water reflects vivid images of my mind,
memories last of loves woven path through bygone days,
I smile and my heart lifts a sigh of nostalgia.
So vivid, so vivid!

The sun blinds me yet warms me within its rays,
encouraged I feel within its comforting embrace,
I see my memories vividly float by on the watery swell.
So encouraging, so encouraging!

I pack my thoughts and to the hills I roam,
loving memories countenanced and emotions stored,
My heart is at peace and my mind at rests.
So loving, so loving!

So sweet, so endearing, so vivid they be.
So encouraging and loving,
The reflections of my memories are to me!

XIII The Mockingbird Sings a Sultry Tune
(As the Bully Preys Upon Their Quarry)

The scoffer rallies his or her brethren around
Like a shepherd rounding up their flock
They knave and prepare their knavish tricks
The sour-faced scoffer and their motley band prey on their fix

Like the jay or cuckoo lays opportune in wait
To instil disaster on the unsuspecting bluebird awaits
The scoffer as a mockingbird hovers and waits
Awaiting to dive and ruffle feathers beneath

Their quarry be not frail nor faltered
But rather knows the moral supremacy they hold
Countenancing their every slight
The meek stand firmly resolved and upright

The scoffer or bully — call them what you wish
Only reigns at your will
Their ridicule and little lives
Mean nothing against to which you may rise

XIV As I Grow Older

As I grow older and look back on bygone days
The faces I've seen and the places I've been
They never fade

As I grow older life stops giving and may take away
The passions I've held and the things I've done
They never pass away

As I grow older and life matures
The loves I've held melt away
They hold memories that remain my comfort and stay

As I grow older I feel my way
The lamentable I consider and the endearing I reflect
They are my life and what I have made

As I grow older and wake each day
The new dawn brings new challenges and hope my way
They are memories that will always stay

As I grow older I grow richer by the day
The knowledge and wisdom I've gained
They are the riches of life and they never fade away

XV Guiding Star

Wither you go; *'quo vadis'*, alas!
You must search, for the path you take.

A guiding star may enchant your way!
Be it folly or fate, you'll follow destiny's way.

You were made to fulfil what life has in store!
We may plan and direct, but fate has the key to the door.

You were born to fill a space!
So make your hallmark in this case, whether you want to or whether
you don't, you have to accept what's in store.

Who you are and what you become!
It's but destiny's plot unique and unsung,
you may search destiny's path, and mould ideas that may fade into
dust.

We have our own purpose in life — each and every one!
Love is a wondrous thing but happiness is the greater one,
just do your best no one can ask more,
and life's plan will chart the way to destiny's door.

XVI Don't Quit!

Don't quit when nothing seems to fit
Don't frown when you're feeling down
Don't despair when all seems up in the air
Do close your eyes and count to ten
Then open them and start again

Just think of the positive
And the negative takes flight
There is that cloud that's silver-lined
However long the road may seem

When things seem so bad
Stand back and take a look
Don't haste or stress nor plummet too
Nor in self-indulgence slump an hour or two

Pick up the pieces
Take stock and start again
Put on a brave smile armed with heart and soul
Don't give in you're too precious to fade

To have tried is but failure turned inside out
You've learnt a lesson called wisdom
The sunset of one day and all it holds Is but the sunrise of another to start anew

Don't give in!

XVII The Last Waltz

Youthful lustre
That once I possessed
Now bottled up in an old chest
Still it shines young at heart
Urging me on to transgress
Older and wiser and mature I've become
But zest for life and youthful charm still holds on
Each hour, each day and each year I gaily play
Cherishing each minute that comes my way
As the serenade comes to close
And as the last waltz plays
I leave the party at its height
As the curtain falls on my last night

XVIII My Beautiful Place

The bright crystal dewdrops in the grass
The sun spits a sunburst high in the sky
The dreamy white clouds float softly by
The perfect place
My beautiful place

Summer's fragrances in the air
Sparrow hops from here to there
Sounds of play faintly heard
Silence surrounds me
My beautiful place

Loving doves flutter and coo
Ladybird bright red on laurel adieu
Lavender lingers in crisp surround
Lazy days beckon
My beautiful place

Whether I go west or ~~to~~ east
Walk or wonder to my ease
Wistful and wonderous is this place
Why I call it
My beautiful place

My heart beats in rhythm
To every contenting sigh
My smile mirrors my happiness
And here I lie
 My beautiful place

XIX Moving On

Fifty years now in this house I've lived
Ten as a boy
Ten as a youth
And the rest I've made my best

My family
My memories
My cheer and heartache too
Within these walls they've all won through

And now a new chapter in my life
I turn a page on a dying light
Horizons anew I reluctantly face
Onward I press to start afresh

Memories dear as the heart is strong
Life's store unfolds yet a new song
New surrounds and friends appear
Nothing's left behind because I'm still me of old

Love and Passion

XX Yearning Siren of Sin

As the rustic shades of Autumn leaves
adorn the dew-soaked ground,
so does my tempest adorn my heart.

With sprit'd passion of furtive energy
my otherwise dormant state,
ooze like a volcanic eruption.

As the virginity of nature cascades around me
my pulse increases as my heart does race,
so like the energy of the water upon the weir.

So do my lustful senses deep within
as a pulsating yearning fighting to breathe,
wanton to feast upon carnal temptation.

With erotic desire I devour the soul
caress the porcelain-like skin against my breast,
with every breath I sweat lustfully ever more.

Until my desire and ardour gives way
until I succumb to this devil within,
my fertile yearning does still grow.

The fair smile of my love adorns me
an artistic body lies before me,
have I loved more, or could I love more?

Hormonal neurosis sets in as my desire retires
but the passion still ferments deep within,
I behold my lover, my siren of sin.

Lest temptations call or with reluctance release
this wanton love for a nuptial kind,

my heart beats against my lover's lustful breast.
My arms with sweet caress engulf my
love with sensual embrace,
my heart and mind akin,
never to lose this love yearning deep within.

XXI Two Hearts Wed

Love's deep caress
Burning within
Love's deep passion
Blossoms us akin
Two as one
For good or for worse
Our hearts are intertwined
With every verse
Wed together
Two as one
We share our lives
Through storm and song
As the years pass
Our hearts embrace
The vows we made
And the love we gave
Not to put asunder
Our precious bond
Nor nip the flame
Our love is built on

Environment and Humanity

XXII Thin Ice

The ice-blue sky
Over the shimmering waters cast a sheen
The sun's bright rays upon the pure white ice
Cast as spectacular scene

A land so plentiful
And seemingly serene
Yet not is all what it seems
In fact quite cereal

Beneath the shedding ice
Waters rise below
The life that lives above
Wither it goes

As the icecap melts and poles disappear
The polar bear of the north struggles to hunt a seal
As the climate changes and greenhouse gases congeal
Upon the carcass of a caribou the fox scrounges a scant meal

As the sun beats down
The albedo effect kicks in
The penguins to the South
Find their home growing ever thin

Fish stocks move as temperatures change
Life's natural cycle plummets into a daze
Where vast snowy plateaus once called home
Floral turfs are now strewn

Ignorantly blissful of his own remiss
Ignorance reverts to play man the fool
For man in the end will endanger himself
Be his own folly at the world's expense

XXIII Peace

Love, hope and pain, the teardrop holds.
Fortitude fights fatigue,
within the displaced soul.

Which is the gem among Courage, hope and love,
hope is the gem, for it possesses them all.
Hope, hell stops and let's light in,
hope, hearts yield and cast aside tyranny and sin.

I look all around and suffering, toil, and despair I see,
the trauma of war and the despair it breeds.
But still a heart beats free with passion and belief,
resolved to hold fast and discount defeat.

Belief that war will end and suffering scatter,
belief that man will reach out and peace matter.
As the conflict grows, my courage grows too,
I pray, I hope, in earnest for my aggressor's soul too.

The bombs they fall around me,
casting devastation and sorrow.
But as I look out with my tear-soaked eyes,
I pretend they're olive leaves floating down from on high.

Through the terror, my hope hangs on,
my hope that peace will reign once more.
That man's hand will reach out,
that olive leaf I so long for.

For despair would be my defeat,
and my hope my strength.
My faith will be my fortress,
to my sacrifice end.

Through the darkness,
a light appears to dry my tears.
Through the darkness,
my olive leaf of peace nears.

General

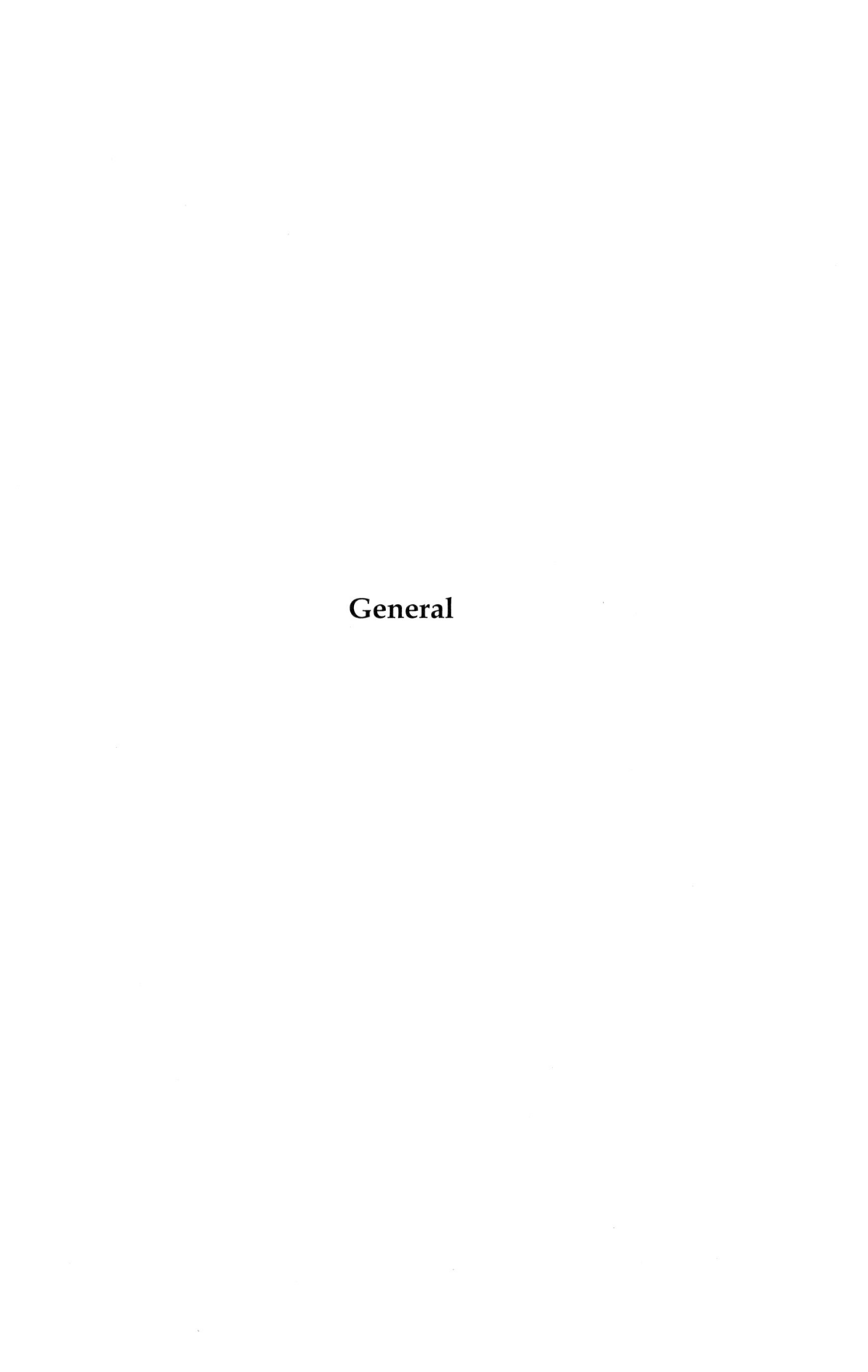

XXIV A Winter Night's Tale

The stars twinkle bright,
in the midnight sky.
The pearl white moon,
shines on high.

Knock, knock, a knocking,
comes the door.
Hoot, hoot, a hooting,
the old owl calls.

The trees ever still,
in the moon's bright beam.
Their twigs reach out,
 like witch's fingers and I scream.

Snuggled up safe,
in my bed I lie.
Snuggled up safe,
safely away.

No knock comes,
nor hoot I hear.
But only ghouls of the mind,
playing games I fear.

It is the winter night,
beckoning out there.
Beckoning my imagination,
to go spare.

All is calm,
all is at peace.
All is as it should be,
and now I'll go to sleep.

XXV The Parish Meeting

Stage is set
For the monthly meet
Clerk enters stage right
All prim and files neat
The usual suspects gather
On council benches and gallery alike
'Councillor grim' resides in his usual site
Scorning a familiar sultry slight
Awaiting the seven o'clock chime
Ready to take their bite of the cake
The mayor's gavel comes down
And the battle lines are set
The usual suspects steal the agenda, hey! hey!
Biting and barking
Along the way
A casual vacancy may arise
As the dust goes up
Heav'n help us
What a bust-up
As the dust starts to settle
And the gavel comes down
It's all over again
We can all go home now and have a dram

XXVI Morning Train

Up at six for the bathroom rush
We yawn and stretch
And rise from our quilt with a push
Eggs and sausage cook
As the toast burns to dust
Dad's clean shirt airs on the side
As the letterbox clatters as the newspaper arrives
Radio blurts out
And television deafens all
Textbook's scramble and school bags fill
Coffee-stained files and crossword half filled
To meet the school bus or dad's eight o'clock train is a dash
Another weekday morning
Which each day we face

XXVII The Green Wood

Deep in the green wood
The wolf howls his call
Deep in the green wood
The bluebells grow tall
Deep in the green wood
The fern blankets the floor
Deep in the green wood
Pinecones litter galore
Deep in the green wood
Owl casts down an eye
Deep in the green wood
Stoat scurries by
Deep in the green wood
Fox lays sleigh and shy
Deep in the green wood
Badger rummages through leaves nearby
Deep in the green wood
The deer graze hither
Deep in the green wood
Dark the green canopy
Spreads out high above
Deep in the green wood
Deep deep deep

XXVIII Birds at Play

Woodpigeon observes from wooden post aloft
Blackbird sings from telephone wires that crisscross
Starling sprightly moves in for some bread
Sparrow bobs from hedge to hedge
With robin both great tit and blue tit play
Whilst cuckoo in tree secreted away

Jenny wren moves like lightning here and there
Goldcrest eats berries left on a chair
Magpie sounds his bittersweet cry
Dunnock camouflaged in buddleia nearby
Chaffinch and goldfinch colourful they be
Display their grace for all to see

XXIX Purring Puss

Purring puss snoozing away
Curled up and snug by the doorway
No care of time he gives a thought
Nor heed to movement through the porch door
But though he sleeps
He's aware of all around
And misses not a trick in his surround
With each purr and one eye all but shut
He discretely scours for ambush
He sits content on his mat
Curled up and snug
Lies little puss

XXX Camelot

Fair Guinevere and mystic Merlin take their place,
at Camelot's court within Arthur's embrace,
'tis the place of honour and grace.

So, hear the tale of this place…

Camelot, this amphitheatre of chivalric tale!
Camelot where gallant knights bid homage,
where noble quests and a crown was made.

Arthur, of Uther's spawn, does sit enthroned at Camelot!
Arthur's banner of Pendragon flies over its mighty walls,
where court is held and knights around a table meet.

Lancelot, king's lieutenant and friend!
Lancelot in his quest for the grail commend,
holds the king's trust at the round table each day.

Gawain, gallant knight of maid and pauper alike!
Gawain brave and courteous was he,
true to his king and destiny.

Geraint, bold knight and prince!
Geraint whose hawk on crest aloft,
rides into battle brave spirit does go.

Percival, hail saviour of Excalibur!
Percival, loyal knight and friend,
to king his service and grail his quest, unto his rest.

Kay, King Arthur's foster kin!
And sound knight through thick and thin,
he sits with pride by Arthur's side.

Galahad, the perfect knight!
Who by God's charge was the grail knight,
son of Lancelot, strong and true, noble and loyal
and a swordsman too.

Tristram, champion of Cornwall and Arthur's good friend true!
Tristram whose chivalry shone through,
with knight's companion he took his place to serve his king with loyal embrace.

XXXI Merry Men of Sherwood

Robin Hood bold and brave in Lincoln green
Noble in spirit and humble at heart
Sets the scene on Sherwood's pastures green
Loathed by the rich and lauded by the poor
Scourge of Nottingham's high sheriff
Guy of Gisbourne too

With dear sweetheart Marian aside
Shadows Sherwood in his stride
Merry men at arms are they
Little John, Much, Will Scarlet and Friar Tuck
With Robin's greater band of warrior bandits be
They thwart Prince John and man is set free

As ballads of olde are told
This is one of chivalry
Charity and conflict pair
Unity amongst despair
To tell the tale of Robin's men
Is one of brotherhood and dare

XXXII Exam Fever

Reading, revision and hazy vision,
no time for social play.
Books and discs and computer chips,
my mind's boggling away.

Exam fever's here and nothing is clear,
except pressure for an AAA.
Do I swat more as my eyes grow sore,
or leave it to fate and do no more?

One thing is for sure, I've given it my all,
and this is no time to turn it in.
So come hell and high water or champers galore,
it's now either sink or swim!

XXXIII The Highwayman

Like diamonds in the sky the stars do flicker,
the full moon casts down it's gentle light upon the vista.
The spooky silhouette of the tree's bandy branches house old owl,
by the random sighs of his old nag the rake lays wait.

But for old owl's hoot silence stay,
the rake listens for sound so patiently still.
Romantic is the night,
so serene until he meets his prey.

With the crunching of stone and the rattling of wheel,
the unsuspecting traveller nears.
Coach thunders forth and in ignorance it nears,
to the fate that waits to reave it so dear.

Weaver by day and reaver by night,
he charges his horse forth into the moonlight.
Flintlock cocked and pistol at the ready,
quarry halts and the moonraker rakes.

Marauding these fair Downs,
he makes haste and gallops away.
With errant spoils,
he makes his way.

How romantic it sounds,
how enchanting the tale.
The moral here be an illicit one,
whilst the reaver makes hay.